HOW NARENDRA MODI IS TRANSFORMING INDIA

YOUTH, MINORITIES AND WOMEN

Dr. AYUSH MISHRA

CONTENTS

Title Page

Copyright

Dedication

Introduction

Preface

                                    1

Brief Life History

Transformation Of India   5

YOUTH   6

Case Study-1 transformation of youth   9

MINORITIES   12

Case study - 2 transformation of minorities   14

WOMEN   16

Case Study -3 transformation of Women   19

Books In This Series   23

INTRODUCTION

Never in the history of independent India people have displayed as much trust in a leader as is being demonstrated in the present prime minister of India.

Narendra Modi is not just a Prime Minister, but a source of encouragement for the common folk and rulers all over the world.

Starting from an extremely modest environment, he has achieved so much that it is a matter of envy for even the world's most influential leaders.

PREFACE

This is the first part of the series of short books on how PM Narendra Modi is transforming India into a modern superpower and Atmanirbhar nation.

This part of the series concentrates on the policies and programmes of Modi government and their effect on youth, minorities, and women.

BRIEF LIFE HISTORY

Birth And Childhood

Narendra Modi was born to Damodardas Modi and Hiraben Modi on 17 September 1950. His father used to sell tea at a station on the railway.

Many difficulties and struggles have faced him since his childhood, but he has turned all the challenges into opportunities.

Modi helped his father sell tea at the railway station in Vadnagar when he was a child, and later ran a tea stall with his brother.

Modi heard about the Rashtriya Swayamsevak Sangh (RSS) when he was eight years old and began to engage in its local shakhas. As per tradition, when they were adolescents, he was married to Jashodaben Chimanlal Modi. .He left home sometime thereafter; the couple lived separate lives. Neither of them married again.

Years Of Self-Discovery

He spent two years traveling across Northern and North-East India, visiting Belur Math near Kolkata after giving up his home, followed by the Advaita Ashrama in Almora and the Ramakrishna

Mission in Rajkot. Vivekananda profoundly inspired him.

Education

Despite hard conditions, Modi strived to receive good education. He had a wonderful ability to pick up concepts and also to reconstruct such concepts for the social good.

In 1967, he completed his higher education in Vadnagar. He obtained a Bachelor of Arts degree in political science from the University of Delhi in 1978, and a Master of Arts degree in political science from the University of Gujarat in 1983.

Through education he happened to appreciate the relevance of ideals of democracy, fraternity, secularism, social welfare, women's empowerment, political and economic rights. It was education which taught him the significance of courage, compassion and consistent hard work.

He had a fondness for deliberations, and an interest to read books.

Political Career

He became an all-time prakharak for the RSS after the Indo-Pakistani War of 1971. He joined the BJP in 1985. In 1988, he became the organizing secretary of the Gujarat Unit of the Party. He was appointed BJP National Secretary in November 1995. He became General Secretary of the BJP in May 1998.

In 2001, for the 1st time, he became Chief Minister of Gujarat and held the office until 2014. He made a fundamental change in administration in Gujrat through his pro-people and pro-active good governance.

He was elected the 14th Prime Minister of India on 26 May 2014. He took the oath as the 15th Prime Minister of India on 30 May 2019,

Awards And Honours

2016-honored with the Order of Abdulaziz Al Saud, Saudi Arabia's highest civil distinction.

2016-honored by the State Order of Ghazi Amir Amanullah Khan, Afghanistan's highest civilian distinction.

2018-honored with the State of Palestine Grand Collar; Palestine's highest civilian distinction for foreign dignitaries .

2018-awarded the Champions of the Earth Award; the highest environmental distinction of the United Nations.

2018-conferred for his contribution to global cooperation and promoting international economic development with the Seoul Peace Prize for 2018.

2019-The Zayed Trophy, the highest civilian decoration in the UAE.

2020 -He was awarded the 'Legion of Merit' by the US on 21 December 2020.

TRANSFORMATION OF INDIA

Let us look at different sectors and sections of economy and society which are being transformed by Narendra Modi government

YOUTH

Modi recognizes India as a country with a glorious future because of its huge demographic surplus. India is one of the youngest nation in the world in terms of demography, and Modi sees it as India's biggest resource. The Modi government has introduced various schemes, policies, and programs that seek to transform youth from work-seeking unemployed men and women to job giving entrepreneurs.

This is the Modi mantra for making India an economic growth center and focuses on four 'E's: education, employment, entrepreneurship, and youth development excellence.

Many Indian young people have received industry-relevant skill training through programs such as Skill India Mission, Skills Acquisition and Knowledge Awareness for Livelihood Promotion (SANKALP, Skills Strengthening for Industrial Value Enhancement (STRIVE), NAPS -National Apprenticeship Promotion Scheme and Pradhan Mantri Kaushal Vikas Yojana (PMKVY) to help them secure a better livelihood.

In order to improve entrepreneurship, the start-up India, stand-up India and Make in India scheme have taken comprehensive steps. The policy strategy is to build an investment-friendly environment, develop modern, productive infrastructure and open up new sectors to foreign investment.

The initiative targeted 25 sectors of the economy to build jobs and develop skills, and aimed to turn India into a global hub for design and manufacturing.

The 'Make In India' project focuses not only on production, but also on the sectors of services and infrastructure. Because of MUDRA, 24 crore loans worth over 10.4 Lakh crore were disbursed to small entrepreneurs and 51 lakh new entrepreneurs were established. 11 crore jobs in the MSME sector were produced. We have noted a trend towards these MSMEs being formalized.

Within a decade, the National Manufacturing Program aims to create 100 million jobs. The policy gives Small-Scale Businesses special attention as it offers job opportunities across different geographies for both self-employment and employment.

Employees Provident Fund Organisation (EPFO) data shows that in infrastructure development projects such as rail, road and airports, lakhs of formal jobs have been generated every year.

These skillilling, reskilling and upskilling programs are not only essential to Atma Nirbhar Bharat, but will also help young people remain active in the job market.

This will result in the masses' increased wages and living conditions resulting in alleviating poverty. As influenced by PM Modi's Local for Vocal call, young people are now becoming self-reliant.

All this, as determined by PM Modi, will help India become an economy of 5 trillion by 2024-25.

"Skill is something which we give to ourselves, skill is a treasure.

Skill is self reliance, makes one not only employable but self employable. Skill is not only a way to earn. It is also a driving force,"

PM MODI

CASE STUDY-1
TRANSFORMATION OF YOUTH

Let Us Look At The Example Of Rahul

Rahul was a young boy of 21 years age in a metropolitan area of North India. He passed his intermediate exam but could not study further because of his father's ill health.

He had to to take care of his family of five including his father, mother and 2 minor sisters.

He used to work at a cycle shop as he couldn't discover any better opportunity. As the earning was less, they could barely satisfy their everyday needs, such as house rental and grocery expenditure. His sisters could not go to school. Though they wanted to study and become physicians, they could not afford the school fee, and so they dropped out of school just like their brother. His father could not receive appropriate treatment owing to a shortage of funds.

He was very anxious about his family's future. Although they could just sustain in the meagre earning, if any stressful condition comes they would be in huge trouble because being in the informal sector he received no benefits like gratuity, insurance, medical facilities etc. There was no job guarantee and he was in uncertainty of losing his work.

 His work condition was also very hectic. Despite working hard for twelve to fourteen hours a day , he could bring in only 7000 a month.

After Coming Of Modi Government, His Condition Improved A Lot.

One day he saw a poster regarding the Pradhan Mantri Skill Development Scheme, which was launched to impart skills to the youth.He went to the local Skill Development Kendra and joined the course of a motor mechanic.

 The course was of 1-year period and was concerned with practical training along with on-the-job training in a big enterprise. He also received a stipend of 10000 rupees during the course.

 He completed the course with full sincerity and devotion. After concluding the course; he got a skill certificate from the government.

 Based on this certificate he got a placement in a motor company with salary twenty thousand a month. His new job was of 8 hours duration with perks like holidays, insurance and medical facilities, pension fund contribution, gratuity, etc.

 He was now assured of his job.His siblings started studying and are preparing for Medical entrance test. He could not study much because of family conditions, but now his sisters could now pursue their dreams. His father's treatment was now taken care by the Employee State Insurance Corporation.

Within two years he constructed own house through his savings and aid from Pradhan Mantri AWAS Yojana(Urban).

He is now reassured of a brilliant future - both of himself and the nation.

Millions of young boys and girls have experienced this kind of revolution through schemes like this.

Thanks to the Prime Minister of India.

MINORITIES

The slogan of Sabka sath sabka vikas by PM Modi has been successful in gaining the confidence of minorities. Modi government has spent Rs 22,000 crore on minority welfare so far and has helped Muslim craftworkers and artisans under the USTTAD scheme

The government has started various schemes to bring down unemployment percentage of minorities,update traditional skills, market linkages, improve employability and empowerment of minority women such as Pradhan Mantri Jan Vikas Karyakram, Jiyo Parsi Scheme , Nai Roshni, Nai Manzil, Usttad, Nai Udaan, Seekho Aur Kamao And Mahila Samriddhi Yojana.

 Modi government encouraged Muslim girls to pursue higher education, and those having graduate degrees have got MAEF scholarships.

Under Modi's rule, there have been scholarships for more than four crore minority children. Drop-out rates have declined among girls from minority groups. Their presence in central government employment has gone up to 10%. Many from the minority groups have been selected for the civil services in the last few years.

Over the last five years, the Jiyo Parsi Scheme implemented to control the declining Parsi population has resulted in 214 births through assisted reproductive techniques (ART).

"Be it caste or communal violence, they stall the growth of the nation. Let us affirm that we will be free from these tensions."
- PM MODI

CASE STUDY - 2
TRANSFORMATION
OF MINORITIES

Let Us Look At The Example Of Razia

Razia was a married woman with 2 children. She was educated but as per tradition her character was restricted to take care of her offspring and family alone. Her life was limited to her home, and she knew nothing about the outside world.

Men took all the significant decisions of her household . She had no voice in the crucial decisions regarding her and the children.

 In the political realm too her voting preference was influenced by her spouse. Transformation of her life

After Coming Of The Modi Government, Her Story Changed A Lot.

She was provided with the information, tools and strategies for engaging with government agencies, banks and other institutions at all levels through programs such as "Nai Roshni", a Leadership Development Programme for Minority Women. It inspired her and instilled confidence in her.

She now has a say in her household in all important decisions. She became aware of many of the community's activities. She is also now voting in the political arena by her preference.

She began to develop awareness of the region's problems and of women in particular. She contested the local body election and is now a ward councillor .

She is also working to encourage other women to learn leadership skills. This includes her neighbors from other groups as well. These then empower other women in a chain response that results in women from the entire community being empowered.

 Thus Razia has now transformed herself into a role model of women and minority empowerment. Million of other men and women from the minority community have transformed their lives through the initiatives of the Modi government.

WOMEN

In India, women in almost all fields, including social, political and economic fields, have historically been less empowered and autonomous than men.

The Modi government has acknowledged the contribution of women to the economy of the country. The government believes that unless the women of the country advance, the country will not progress.

Government has introduced schemes such as Standup India, Pradhan Mantri Mudra Yojna (PMMY), Pradhan Mantri Jan-Dhan Yojana (PMJDY), Atal Pension Yojana (APY), Pradhan Mantri Jeevan Jyoti Bima Yojana (PMJJBY) and Pradhan Mantri Suraksha Bima Yojana (PMSBY) to empower women economically. They motivate them to lead a better life and fulfill their dreams of becoming an entrepreneur.

These schemes have generated fruit. Under the 'Stand Up India' program, women now account for over 81 percent of the overall beneficiaries. Under PM Jan Dhan Yojana, as many as 19,86 crore women Jan Dhan accounts were opened for the financial inclusion of women.
The goal of Pradhan Mantri Ujjwala Yojana (PMUY) is to resolve serious health hazards associated with non-fossil fuel-based cooking. Under the Ujjwala Yojana over 11.97 crore LPG cylinders

have been issued for free.

Under this system, the LPG connections and the electricity connections under Pradhan Mantri Saubhagya Yojana are given in the name of women. It is an effort to give them a sense of ownership. It is also a recognition of their right to property which was traditionally denied to them.

Modi's Beti Bachao Beti Padhao system seeks to prevent gender discriminatory sexual abortion, ensure the girl's child's survival & safety, and ensure the girl's child's education. This system seems to have been a huge success and has led to a change of attitude towards the girl child along with initiatives such as the "SELFIE WITH DAUGHTER" initiative. Parents do not look at them as a burden anymore. The gap between a boy and a girl child in the psyche is quickly dying out. In urban areas, the sex ratio at birth rose from 922 in 2011-12 to 965 in 2017-18.

A savings scheme introduced as part of the Beti Bachao, Beti Padhao campaign is Sukanya Samriddhi Yojana (SSY). This system allows guardians to open a savings account with an approved commercial bank or branch of India Post for their girl child. The scheme has seen an impressive achievement of 54,000 crore deposits.

Launched by the Ministry of Health & Family Welfare, the Pradhan Mantri Surakshit Matritva Abhiyan aims to provide cost-free, assured, comprehensive and quality prenatal care to all pregnant women on the 9th of every month.

Launched in 2017, PMMVY (Pradhan Mantri Matru Vandana Yojana) provides all pregnant women and lactating mothers with cash benefits of Rs 6000 as compensation for the loss of wages during pregnancy. This encourages them to relax and thereby minimizes the risks associated with pregnancy.

The One Stop Center and the Crisis hotline for Women help women report crimes such as abuse and seek free legal assistance. The goal of the UJJAWALA scheme is to provide comprehensive support for women impacted by violence (medical, legal, psychological, etc.) and to prevent trafficking in women and children.

"Our Matru Shakti is our pride. Women empowerment is very crucial to our development."

-PM Modi

CASE STUDY -3 TRANSFORMATION OF WOMEN

Let Us Look At The Story Of Sudha.

Sudha was born in a poor farmer family in Eastern India. She could not study and was married at a very tender age. She used to cook food on a chullah and suffered discomfort in eyes and cough because of the smoke.

Her Husband was educated till Primary only and so could not get any good job .He used to work as a daily wage labourer at five thousand a month. He had a small piece of land but couldn't till it due to lack of investment and irrigation facilities.

They used to go to the fields for defecation as they had no toilet in their kaccha house. They had no electricity connection.

They lead a very poor lifestyle because of less earning. They were being provided government benefits like subsidised ration. But those were not effective because of huge leakage and corruption.

In the time of adversity such as illness they had no option but to sell their land or ornaments or to borrow at a high rate from the local moneylenders as they could not get loans from the banks. They had no bank accounts even.

After Coming Of Modi Government, Their Life Changed A Lot.

Both Sudha and her husband got free bank account opened with atm facility through the Pradhan Mantri Jan Dhan Yojana.

Sudha got a free LPG connection through Pradhan Mantri Ujjwala Yojana and became free from the harmful smoke of the chullah and saved time, which was wasted in collecting firewood. She spent this time in taking care of her child and other productive pursuits. She also got a free electricity connection through Pradhan Mantri Saubhagya Yojana.

Through the Pradhan Mantri Krishi Sinchai Yojana irrigation facility reached their village. They also got six thousand rupees credited to their bank account through the Pradhan Mantri Kisan Samman Nidhi and started cultivating their own land. Their harvest was also insured for any kind of pre or post harvest damage through the Pradhan Mantri Fasal Bima Yojana of the government.

They receive all their subsidies and other government benefits directly in their bank accounts with no intermediary. because of AADHAR seeding corruption in food subsidy was eliminated and they now get ration at regular intervals.

They also took a loan of two lakhs through Pradhan Mantri MUDRA Yojana and set up a small food processing plant on their own farmland. They sourced raw material from the village farmers. The final product was sent to a supermarket in a nearby town.

The payments were done through the bank account and BHIM mobile payment facility launched by the government. Extra produce could be sold through e National Agriculture Market facility to anywhere in India.

Now they could earn Thirty thousand a month. They also gave employment to five women. They constructed their pucka house through Pradhan Mantri Awas Yojana and they got their own toilet by Pradhan Mantri Swachchhta Abhiyan.

During the first pregnancy, Sudha did not see any doctor and her daughter was born at the home.But this time she got free Ante Natal checkups through the Pradhan Mantri Surakshit Matritva Abhiyan.

She also got six thousand rupees through the Pradhan Mantri Matru Vandana Yojana.She delivered a healthy child in a government hospital free.

Her mother-in-law got her bile stone removal surgery done in a private hospital without any fee through the Pradhan Mantri Ayushman Yojana, including the cost of medicines .

She was married at a tender age but her daughter would not have the same fate .Thanks to the Pradhan Mantri Sukanya Samriddhi Yojana - A small investment scheme launched by PM Modi .

It would ensure a handsome sum for her education when she becomes 18 years old. Thus she could fulfill all her dreams, which Sudha could not.

After reading this story, nobody would doubt that PM Modi has brought a complete transformation of life of women and empowered them.

BOOKS IN THIS SERIES

HOW PM MODI IS TRANS-FORMING INDIA

THE SERIES FOCUSES DIFFEFRENT SECTORS AND SECTIONS OF ECONOMY AND SOCIETY WHICH ARE BEING TRANSFORMED BY NARENDRA MODI GOVERNMENT

How Pm Modi Is Transforming India - Part 1

THIS PART OF THE SERIES   FOCUSES ON THE POLICIES AND PROGRAMMES OF MODI GOVERNMENT AND THEIR EFFECT ON YOUTH , MINORITIES AND WOMEN